ADORE

A GUIDED ADVENT JOURNAL FOR PRAYER AND MEDITATION

FR. JOHN BURNS

ILLUSTRATED BY VALERIE DELGADO

AVE MARIA PRESS AVE Notre Dame, Indiana

© 2021 by Ave Maria Press, Inc.

All rights reserved. No part of this book may be used or reproduced in any manner whatsoever, except in the case of reprints in the context of reviews, without written permission from Ave Maria Press®, Inc., P.O. Box 428, Notre Dame, IN 46556, 1-800-282-1865.

Founded in 1865, Ave Maria Press is a ministry of the United States Province of Holy Cross.

www.avemariapress.com

Paperback: ISBN-13 978-1-64680-119-0

E-book: ISBN-13 978-1-64680-120-6

Cover and interior images © 2021 Valerie Delgado, paxbeloved.com.

Cover and text design by Brianna Dombo.

Printed and bound in the United States of America.

CONTENTS

INTRODUCTION

BEHOLD,
I MAKE ALL THINGS NEW.

REVELATION 21:5

Each of us carries a deep longing to be made new. That longing is a fundamental part of our humanness. We live it rhythmically as we mark the passing of time—for example, with the changing of the calendar every January. The new year often brings resolutions to become better at what matters most, to refocus, to make changes. Even though our resolutions often crumble, the repeated effort of making them speaks to our aching desire to be better and our attempts to become so.

In an even deeper manner, the Catholic faith is marked to its very core by God's ceaseless invitation to begin anew. For the believer, each year is interwoven with the movements of the liturgical seasons, the repetition of which perpetually draws us more and more deeply into life in Christ. In secular terms, the new year begins in January. But on the spiritual plane, our new year starts even earlier, with Advent. Advent is, in a real sense, our annual new beginning. It can and should be marked with the same drive to refocus, but on a goal beyond weight loss or picking up a new hobby. Advent is a time to prepare for the Second Coming of Christ, as we remember the first time he came to us and see him come to us again and again.

Of all the seasons of the year, Advent offers us perhaps the clearest sense of adventure and journey. It is a season for resetting our horizon, reframing our movement toward fullness in

Christ. And even though Advent is brief, it is filled with spiritual riches.

Yet, because Advent falls during a busy time of year, we often rush over or even miss the treasures God places before us in the Church. The book you are holding is organized around my desire to lift these gifts up and hold them out to you in a way that deepens your entry into the greatest of mysteries.

Two particular dimensions of our Catholic faith—the flow of the liturgy and the wealth of the devotional life of the Church—will inform our Advent journey as follows:

✦ The readings of the Advent Masses, both during the week and on the weekends, help shape the insights through which our prayer will progress.

✦ The opening prayer of each Mass, called the Collect, often slips by too quickly. The Collects of Advent are especially rich, and these will sit quietly beneath the shape of our journey.

✦ Finally, a few traditional elements of the Church's devotional life further shape our pilgrimage toward Christmas. Traditionally, Wednesdays are devoted to St. Joseph, Thursdays to the Eucharist and the priesthood, Fridays to penance and the Cross, and Saturdays to our Lady, all oriented toward our fuller celebration of the Resurrection on Sunday. In a subtle fashion, these themes will accompany us on our pilgrimage toward Christmas, in a way that will hopefully awaken a rhythm you can carry with you the rest of the year.

My hope is that the pages that follow will help you settle down and enter into a journey that, year after year, promises to transform our lives. We really do set out on an adventure together, as a Church, every year. In this season of longing, hope, and new beginnings, let us move toward a deeper adoration of the

King of kings, who comes in the quiet of the night to save us.
When we engage the movements of the season, we begin to sing
more fully that cherished hymn:

> O come, let us adore him,
> O come, let us adore him,
> O come, let us adore him,
> Christ the Lord.

FR. JOHN BURNS

HOW TO USE
THIS JOURNAL

The *Adore* Advent journal's combination of daily meditations, questions for reflection, journaling space, prayers, and beautiful original art is specially designed to draw you into a deeper, richer experience of Advent, preparing you not only to celebrate Jesus' long-ago arrival in Bethlehem but also to receive and adore him as he continues to arrive today, in the Eucharist and in our hearts.

WHO IS ADORE FOR?

Adore is for anyone who desires Advent to be a time of preparation to receive and adore Jesus wholeheartedly. The holiday season can be a time of great excitement, fun, and happiness, but it can also fill up with busyness and stresses that distract us from the real meaning of Christmas. This Advent journal provides a daily path back to the purpose of the Advent season, orienting you toward the anticipation and celebration of Jesus' arrival.

Adore is perfect for use in a group setting, and was designed with that in mind. There's something special about taking this Advent journey with a community—whether that community is your entire parish, a small group, or your family. Visit **www. avemariapress.com/adore** for information about bulk discounts, a leader's guide, help with organizing a small group, videos from Fr. John Burns discussing the theme for each week of Advent, and other resources to help you make the most of your time together with *Adore*.

You can also use *Adore* as an individual, with the meditations and journaling prompts helping you draw near to God, hear his voice in new ways, and pour out your heart to him as you turn your attention daily to Jesus' imminent arrival. You may find that this Advent you're in special need of regular, quiet times of connection with God; *Adore* is an excellent way to help you find that space each day.

HOW IS ADORE ORGANIZED?

Adore is organized into four weekly themes.

✦ In the first week, you'll focus on the idea of *watchfulness*—developing eyes of faith to see where Jesus is revealing himself and fostering an eagerness to run to him wherever you see him.

✦ The second week's theme is *preparation*; the meditations will help you come to terms with your brokenness and need, while also filling your heart with hope for Jesus' healing presence.

✦ The third week focuses on the concept of *nearness*. Throughout this week you'll be invited to ponder the amazing intimacy of Jesus' presence with his creation through the Incarnation, not only as it was experienced by Mary and Joseph in the months preceding Jesus' birth but also as it is made available in special ways to us today.

✦ The final week celebrates *Emmanuel*, God with us, inviting us to worshipful silence and adoration in the last few days before the celebration of Christmas.

Within each week, you'll encounter a simple daily pattern made up of the following parts:

✦ Each day opens with a *quotation* from a saint, great teacher, or scripture, meant to focus your thoughts on the key idea from that day's meditation.

- ✦ The *meditation* from Fr. John Burns draws out a message from the liturgy, from scripture, or from the experiences of Mary and Joseph as they prepared to welcome the infant Jesus into their lives.

- ✦ The *reflect* section challenges you to ponder and journal in response to the meditation, helping you identify practical ways to live out the Advent season more fully.

- ✦ Finally, after you've read and journaled, the closing *prayer* provides a starting point for your own requests and prayers of thanksgiving and praise to God.

HOW SHOULD I READ ADORE?

This Advent journal's daily format is flexible enough to accommodate any reader's preferences: If you're a morning person, you may want to start your day with *Adore*, completing the entire day's reading, reflection, journaling, and prayer first thing in the morning. Or, you may find that you prefer to end your day by using *Adore* to focus your attention on Christ as you begin to rest from the day's activities. You may even decide to read and pray as a family in the morning and journal individually in the evening.

The key is finding what works for you, ensuring that you have time to read carefully, ponder deeply, write honestly, and connect intimately with the Lord in prayer.

Whatever approach you choose (and whether you decide to experience *Adore* with a group or on your own), be sure to visit **www.avemariapress.com/adore** for extra resources to help you get the most out of this special Advent journey.

FIRST WEEK
OF ADVENT

WATCHFULNESS

FIRST WEEK OF ADVENT

SUNDAY

LET US FLEE FROM THE DECEIT OF LIFE AND ITS SUPPOSED HAPPINESS AND RUN TO CHRIST ALONE, WHO IS THE SAVIOR OF SOULS. HIM LET US ENDEAVOR TO FIND WHO IS PRESENT EVERYWHERE, AND WHEN WE HAVE FOUND HIM LET US HOLD HIM FAST AND FALL AT HIS FEET AND EMBRACE THEM IN THE FERVOR OF OUR SOULS.

ST. SYMEON THE NEW THEOLOGIAN

RUN TO CHRIST

The Sundays of Advent are particularly important because they set the framework for the whole season and offer, for each week, a focal point and banner that stands over the days that follow. The first Sunday of Advent, which begins the whole season, has an undeniably clear message: vigilant watchfulness.

In the gospel, Christ exhorts us to watch, be vigilant, and stay awake. Christ preached these themes because of the danger of their opposites: distraction, carelessness, and spiritual drowsiness. We return to these words of Christ every single year, and on the very first day of the new liturgical year we start fresh in the fervent pursuit of what truly matters. In turn, the fresh start entails the acknowledgment of the many ways we have lost our focus and zeal for the ultimately important ideals of the Gospel.

The Collect from today's Mass places over Advent an energetic, driven resoluteness: "Grant your faithful, we pray, almighty God, the resolve to run forth to meet your Christ with righteous deeds at his coming." The outcry of the Church here is for more than just readiness; it is for fervor, and it is filled with movement. We beg God to help us *run* to Christ.

As our journey toward Christmas takes form today, we set before our hearts that toward which we press: adoration of the King of the universe, who takes up flesh to redeem all of creation and thereby to "make all things new" (Rv 21:5). The more perfectly we worship him, the greater freedom we give to God to transform our lives and bring forth the image of Christ imprinted on our souls by grace. Toward the inbreaking of the kingdom we turn our gaze; for the coming of Christ we maintain vigil; for the presence of God and the signs of his constant presence we watch. This is our Advent.

REFLECT

Stretch beyond a passive readiness for Christ's arrival. What are some ways you can move with fervor and resoluteness toward Christ?

PRAY

*ALMIGHTY GOD, GRANT ME THE
RESOLVE TO RUN TO YOUR SON THIS
ADVENT SEASON, MEETING HIM WITH
A PURE HEART AND GOOD DEEDS.*

FIRST WEEK OF ADVENT

MONDAY

WHEREVER I GO I WILL FIND
YOU, MY GOD.

ST. JEAN-BAPTISTE DE LA SALLE

BE ALERT TO HIS PRESENCE

Have you ever noticed how often Christ called his listeners to attentive, vigilant watchfulness? Perhaps he preached these themes so frequently because he saw our tendency to become drowsy and lethargic, feeble and forgetful. The season of Advent embodies Christ's exhortation in splendid fashion. The Collect from today's Mass is instructive: "Keep us alert, we pray, O Lord our God, as we await the advent of Christ your Son, so that, when he comes and knocks, he may find us watchful in prayer and exultant in his praise."

Alertness, in spiritual terms, is a form of attentiveness, the ability to see past the surface and notice the subtler movements that are so easily lost in busyness and distraction. Spiritual alertness is marked by an interior awareness that God's activity swirls all around us as God's will sustains all that is in existence. Every moment of every day is thick with opportunity for communion. Let that sink in; it means an end to boredom and an opening of life to the infinite and constant possibilities of grace. Our prayer amounts to the imploring request that God would teach us to live an entirely different way, so that we would walk by faith and not by sight (see 2 Corinthians 5:7). What a beautiful possibility that we could live with eyes of faith! Our longing is to become so profoundly aware of God that we might recognize in all things—the good, the bad, the sweet, and the burdensome—some opportunity to respond to and cooperate with the unfolding will of God.

It is simply true that God comes to us throughout each day, in our duties and undertakings. He comes to the door of our hearts to be with us. Christ's promise is this: "If any one hears my voice and opens the door, I will come in to him and eat with him, and he with me." (Rv 3:20). It is a promise almost too beautiful to bear that the God of the universe invites us into such an intimate sharing of life as this. The condition for the gift is simple: that we believe, that we watch in prayer, and that we exult in his praise.

REFLECT

Do you believe that the world around you is full of God's presence and that your life is saturated with opportunities for communion with him? Ponder and write about some ways you can develop eyes to see those opportunities.

_____
_____
_____
_____
_____
_____
_____
_____
_____
_____
_____
_____
_____

PRAY

*ALMIGHTY GOD, I YEARN FOR YOUR
PRESENCE. GRANT ME THE EYES TO
SEE IN MY EVERYDAY MOMENTS,
NO MATTER HOW SMALL, AN
OPPORTUNITY TO UNITE WITH YOU.*

FIRST WEEK OF ADVENT

TUESDAY

SETTLE YOURSELF IN SOLITUDE,
AND YOU WILL ENCOUNTER GOD
IN YOURSELF.

ST. TERESA OF ÁVILA

FROM LONELINESS TO INTIMACY

A watchful heart that looks to the horizon in steady, hopeful expectation is a lasting fruit of a well-lived Advent. *What will this day bring, Lord? What does this moment bear? How will you come into the places of greatest need, both in the world and in my life?*

A watchful heart searches constantly for the Lord and learns to sense God's presence by observation of the fruits of grace. A watchful heart, oriented as it is to the horizon in faith, is also a heart that searches its own depths in fearless confidence. The Carmelite saints have helped believers realize the truth that God dwells in the inner chamber of the soul, at its center. Therefore, a watchful heart seeks the Lord and labors to follow him to the ends of the earth and to the deepest recesses of the soul.

If eyes of faith open our lives to the endless possibilities of interaction with God, putting an end to boredom, the awareness of God's indwelling presence puts an end to loneliness. How often do we stumble through life with a woeful sense of isolation, curling up sorrowfully in our pain as we feel forgotten or cast aside by others? Yet our suffering here is so often the result of narrow vision, and we give it power by treating it as the end of the story. Christ offers a completely different way: "I am with you always," he says to the disciples (Mt 28:20). We are never alone.

This truth changes everything. In faith, loneliness shifts to solitude, and solitude is the perfect place for intimacy with God in the absence of any other distraction or activity. We must allow ourselves to be surprised by the potential of our own hearts, chosen as they are by God to be his dwelling.

REFLECT

Where do you find yourself as you pray today? If you are in a season of loneliness, how might you move from loneliness to solitude? How might you make space for intimacy with God? If your life is full of life-giving relationships, how can you protect and foster your awareness of God's indwelling presence?

PRAY

*LOVING GOD, WHEREVER I FIND
MYSELF TODAY, GRANT ME A LIFE-
GIVING AWARENESS OF YOUR
INTIMATE CLOSENESS.*

FIRST WEEK OF ADVENT

WEDNESDAY

THINK OF THE STEPS OF ST. JOSEPH'S GREATNESS. HE BEGAN BY THE PURE LOVE OF A SPOTLESS VIRGIN. GRADUALLY, AS THE MYSTERY UNFOLDED ITSELF, THE EARTHLY LOVE TURNED TO ENRAPTURED VENERATION, AND MARY BECAME TO HIM A TRUST FROM THE GOD OF HIS FATHERS, A DIVINE TREASURE TO BE GUARDED FROM EVERY SHADOW OF ILL.

JAMES J. McGOVERN, *THE MANUAL OF THE HOLY CATHOLIC CHURCH*

TO SEE WITH
EYES OF FAITH

As we observed in the introduction, Wednesdays are traditionally devoted to St. Joseph, and we invite him in a special way into our movement toward the manger throughout Advent.

St. Joseph learned in a unique way what it means to live in the presence of God and to be moved by the beauty of God's grace. He was granted the singular gift of marriage to the greatest jewel of all of creation, the Blessed Virgin Mary.

In the chaste love that captivated his heart and drew him daily more deeply toward perfect love, he beheld in delighted awe the splendor of a creature unmarred by sin. We can only speculate what it must have been like to see her, to watch her move and live and be. Her presence must have provoked in everyone who knew her a memory of God's original design for humanity and, in the same moment, the whisper of an awareness of our future destiny.

With Mary, God's long-awaited plan was finally set in motion. In faith, Joseph looked upon her in wonder. As a craftsman, Joseph must have had an eye for aesthetics, for beauty, form, harmony, and balance. With eyes of faith, he must have learned of the brilliant perfection of the Father's plan as he beheld Mary, the ark and tabernacle divinely fashioned as a dwelling place for God.

Joseph's eyes rightfully looked upon Mary in exclusive love yet as a man who held the lily of her heart for God in a love both generous and pure. In this way, Joseph's nearness to Mary sculpted his heart for excellence in covenant love. We ask his intercession in a special way through Advent for growth in the same excellence: for eyes of faith, a watchful heart, and a love that is chaste, generous, and strong.

REFLECT

Joseph's love for the Blessed Virgin Mary reveals how human love—spousal, familial, and fraternal—can reflect and participate in divine love. What are some ways you can live out Joseph's example of self-giving, God-oriented love in your own relationships?

_____

_____

_____

_____

_____

_____

_____

_____

_____

_____

_____

PRAY

*ST. JOSEPH, PRAY FOR ME, SO THAT
I MAY LOOK ON THOSE I LOVE WITH
EYES OF FAITH. MAY MY LOVE FOR
THEM REFLECT GOD'S GENEROUS
AND PURE LOVE.*

WHEN I SEE THAT THE BURDEN
IS BEYOND MY STRENGTH, I DO
NOT CONSIDER OR ANALYZE IT
OR PROBE INTO IT, BUT I RUN
LIKE A CHILD TO THE HEART OF
JESUS.

ST. FAUSTINA KOWALSKA

FIND YOUR FOUNDATION

Have you ever noticed that it's precisely when life already feels too busy that something brand new gets added to our list—and nothing can be taken off? In the endless whirlwind of busyness, it can be difficult to know that we're in the right place and on the right track.

Our own history of sin, along with our past mistakes and failures, can add to our feelings of uncertainty, trapping us in a crippling cycle of insecurity. Worse yet, we often encounter these feelings of overwork and anxiety from a place of loneliness. In this anxious race into an uncertain future, with everything shifting around us, we yearn for a solid place to find our footing, a firm foundation.

In the gospel, Jesus reminds us that when we set our foundation on sand, the floods come and wash everything away. But those who listen to Jesus' words are like the wise man who built his house on solid rock. In the arid landscape of the Holy Land, several yards of sand and topsoil cover the deep bedrock. To build on rock did not mean simply finding an outcropping of rock and building there. Rather, it meant taking the time to dig deep, sometimes through many layers of sand and soil, to find a solid foundation suitable for building a house that wouldn't wash away in the storm.

Christ says that the wise one who builds on rock is the one who "hears these words of mine and does them" (Mt 7:24). We can always find comfort and refuge in his words, no matter the trial we are facing:

✢ When we are tired, we hear, "Come to me, all you who labor and are heavy laden, and I will give you rest" (Mt 11:28).

✢ When we feel alone, we hear, "Behold, I am with you always, to the close of the age" (Mt 28:20).

✤ When we feel empty, we hear, "I am the bread of life; he who comes to me shall not hunger, and he who believes in me shall never thirst" (Jn 6:35).

In the Eucharist—at Mass and in adoration—we are always invited to release the burdens we carry, to sweep away the sand and debris and find once again our intimate connection with the God who is our firm foundation.

REFLECT

Is anything coming between you and your attempts to make Jesus the bedrock of your life? Make a list of of these things— daily worries and distractions, past sins and mistakes, unresolved traumas—and offer them up to the Lord.

_____

_____

_____

_____

_____

_____

_____

_____

_____

PRAY

DEAR JESUS, HELP ME CLING TO YOUR PROMISES WHEN I AM NEEDY, ALONE, BURDENED, OR BROKEN: YOU PROVIDE REST. YOU SATISFY MY THIRST. YOU ARE WITH ME. YOU ARE MY FOUNDATION, THE DEEP BEDROCK UPON WHOM I BUILD MY LIFE.

FIRST WEEK OF ADVENT

FRIDAY

WHO EXCEPT GOD CAN GIVE
YOU PEACE? HAS THE WORLD
EVER BEEN ABLE TO SATISFY THE
HEART?

ST. GERARD MAJELLA

MADE FOR INTIMACY

Have you ever experienced a moment when you longed for home but felt far away? When your heart ached for "something more" and you simply could not find rest? In our earthly journey, we discover again and again that the things we think will satisfy us never quite do. In the light of faith, we recognize this as a sign that we were made for an uncreated good, something that lasts forever and is greater than any passing creature.

How easily we forget this fact, though. We enthrone created things and treat them as though they could possibly be the ultimate and finally satisfying good. Whether it be wealth, power, or pleasure, when we treat created goods—even persons—as though they could give final rest to our wandering hearts, we are headed for heartbreak. Only God, the uncreated good, is enough to satisfy the ache of the human heart.

This is why St. Augustine famously cried out, "O God, you have created us for yourself, and our hearts are restless until they rest in you." At the core of our unsettled state are our myriad futile attempts to find rest in created things.

Throughout the year, Friday is meant to be a day of penance and self-denial. We make sacrifices on Fridays to recall Christ's great sacrifice on Good Friday. In part, our sacrifices discipline and test our attachment to created goods. When we deny ourselves little comforts, our suffering sheds light on the many ways we cling too tightly to the offerings of this world.

Mortification leads to self-mastery, a process that purifies our ability to lift our eyes from passing goods and set them instead upon the everlasting good that is God Almighty. Fasting and abstinence throughout the year deepen our commitment to tread the pilgrim pathways of this life with hearts rightly attuned to eternity.

REFLECT

What created things are you tempted to look toward when your heart is restless? Have they ever provided true satisfaction or abiding rest? How might these lesser goods light your path toward the uncreated good that is God?

_____

_____

_____

_____

_____

_____

_____

_____

_____

_____

_____

_____

_____

_____

_____

_____

_____

_____

_____

_____

_____

_____

_____

_____

PRAY

*O GOD, YOU DESIGNED ME TO
EXPERIENCE INTIMACY WITH YOU,
AND I KNOW I WILL NEVER FIND REST
UNTIL I LOOK TO YOU ALONE FOR
ALL THAT MY HEART CRAVES. HELP ME
REST IN YOU TODAY.*

FIRST WEEK OF ADVENT

SATURDAY

LIVE IN FAITH AND HOPE,
THOUGH IT BE IN DARKNESS,
FOR IN THIS DARKNESS GOD
PROTECTS THE SOUL. CAST YOUR
CARE UPON GOD FOR YOU ARE
HIS AND HE WILL NOT FORGET
YOU. DO NOT THINK THAT HE IS
LEAVING YOU ALONE, FOR THAT
WOULD BE TO WRONG HIM.

ST. JOHN OF THE CROSS

HOPE IN THE
VALLEY OF TEARS

Our faith offers a weekly rhythm, and when we settle into it, we find a perpetual movement between fast and feast, as we both curb our appetites and celebrate the gift of creation. Between Friday and Sunday lies a true gem: devotion to our Lady. As Friday places our attention on the Cross, Saturday brings us to the lily that flourishes at its foot: the Blessed Virgin Mary. One of the reasons Saturday is traditionally devoted to Mary is because of the way she bore the hope and heart of the Church on Holy Saturday.

As Christ's body lay in the tomb, we cannot help but ponder the experience of the disciples as despair and fear shook their young faith. Only our Lady, without sin, would have held to the hope in God's promises even when all seemed lost. She thus offers unfailing recourse to all who suffer and toil through what the Salve Regina (Hail, Holy Queen) refers to as "this valley of tears."

Mary's gaze never left the Lord; since the proclamation of the angels at Jesus' birth she had "kept all these things, pondering them in her heart" (Lk 2:19). This pondering heart of Mary, we might speculate, found its deepest mooring in the days of her pregnancy. What would it have been like to receive the words of the angel, to consent to the surprising plan of God, and then to pass nine months with the Second Person of the Trinity enfleshed and hidden within her womb? What subtle splendor, what quiet wonder, what unimaginable blessing! How the indwelling of God must have shaped the rest of her life as it formed her faith to endure the Passion and celebrate the Resurrection.

Mary's watchfulness, her attentive waiting for the birth of the Savior, is especially important for the rest of the Church during Advent. Her vigilant heart is inseparable from the abiding mystery of Christ within, and for this reason we fly to her as our refuge and intercessor. In this first week, we especially strive to focus our attention on the horizon toward which we press. We ask for the grace of a watchful, pondering, tranquil heart that knows, as Mary did, the real presence of God here and now.

REFLECT

Though we experience God's blessing and presence in all kinds of wonderful ways, our earthly lives often feel like that Saturday long ago—the heartbreak of the Cross still fresh and the joy of Resurrection yet to be realized. That is why we are to be vigilant, always on the lookout for Christ's arrival. Reflect here about your experience over the past week using this Advent journal to practice watchfulness. How has it blessed or challenged you?

_____

_____

_____

_____

_____

_____

_____

_____

_____

_____

PRAY

OUR LADY OF HOPE, PRAY FOR ME.
SHARE WITH ME YOUR WATCHFUL,
STEADY, FAITHFUL HEART THAT
KNOWS THE REAL PRESENCE OF GOD
HERE AND NOW. HELP ME LOOK
AHEAD WITH VIGILANT HOPE TOWARD
ALL THAT GOD WILL DO.

SECOND WEEK
OF ADVENT
PREPARATION

SECOND WEEK OF ADVENT

SUNDAY

REPENTANCE IS A CONTRACT
WITH GOD FOR A SECOND LIFE.

ST. JOHN CLIMACUS

NEW LIFE
THROUGH REPENTANCE

The gospel at Mass this weekend speaks with utter clarity about the shape of the week to come: "Prepare the way of the Lord" (Mt 3:3). The Collect of today's Mass undeniably orients us toward the horizon of Christ's coming: "Almighty and merciful God, may no earthly undertaking hinder those who set out in haste to meet your Son." The dynamism of the liturgy is twofold: it elicits both a stable interior preparation to welcome Christ and a concurrent eagerness to run forth when we finally catch sight of "him whom my soul loves" (Sg 3:4).

John the Baptist, an extraordinary biblical figure, stands in the wilderness within this very tension. The great forerunner to Christ and the last of the prophets, he cries out, "Repent, for the kingdom of heaven is at hand" (Mt 3:2). In so doing, he identifies the fundamental change that must occur within, a change that serves both to prepare the heart and bestow the interior agility of one who keeps watch, ready to run toward Christ.

Repentance is both demanding and liberating. It involves admitting the futility of our own attempts to satisfy our needs and wants and embracing the fact of our own poverty. It requires renouncing our attempts to survive outside the framework of God's grace. In simple terms, we say "Help! I cannot do this on my own, and I will no longer try to do so." With contrite hearts, we lament our sinfulness and resolve to leave it behind.

Wonderfully, just when the movement of repentance might seem on the verge of crushing our hearts into despair, we come face-to-face with the unfailing patience, kindness, and mercy of God, who always awaits our return. We lift our hearts toward the Lord, as little children who cry out to their Father. From the Father's love and moved by his Spirit, we welcome Christ's power, authority, and love over our lives.

Repentance is a total change, and when it is sincere, we experience for ourselves the full truth of St. Paul's words: "Therefore, if anyone is in Christ, he is a new creation; the old has passed away, behold, the new has come" (2 Cor 5:17).

REFLECT

Think about a time when you embraced the pain and liberation of genuine repentance. Is there anything you're holding on to that is blocking you from experiencing the newness of life described by St. Paul in 2 Corinthians 5:17?

_____

_____

_____

_____

_____

_____

_____

_____

_____

PRAY

LORD, I KNOW THAT PREPARING FOR YOUR ARRIVAL MEANS REPENTING OF ALL THE THINGS THAT COME BETWEEN YOU AND ME. HELP ME EMBRACE THE DEMAND—AND EXPERIENCE THE FREEDOM—OF TRUE REPENTANCE THIS WEEK OF ADVENT.

SECOND WEEK OF ADVENT

MONDAY

THERE IS NO JOY LIKE THAT
KNOWN BY THE TRULY POOR IN
SPIRIT.

ST. THÉRÈSE OF LISIEUX

BEGGARS BEFORE
A GENEROUS GOD

At the core of repentance is the humble recognition that we cannot save ourselves. Try as we might, we will never achieve by our own power the type of happiness for which we so desperately long. St. Augustine famously said, "Man is a beggar before God." When we accept this truth and enter that space to cry out in need, it is as though we grant God permission to do as he wishes within us. While God's strength is not curbed by our closed hearts, in his kindness, his love is never forced. God patiently waits for us to welcome his power.

The power of God is especially manifested in healing, whereby God's gift of grace restores us to an order and integrity that underlies the disorder and chaos we so often experience in our interior lives. In our anguished confusion, every attempt to medicate and cover over our wounds only further agitates the sorrow and suffering within. The landscape of our heart becomes a dry and parched land. The weight of our inner pain cripples us.

Such is the condition of the soul in its poverty, and through the prophets God speaks directly into this poverty with a promise: "The wilderness and the dry land shall be glad, the desert shall rejoice and blossom; like the lily it shall blossom abundantly, and rejoice with joy and singing" (Is 35:1–2).

Advent is the end of a long history of waiting for the fulfillment of an ancient promise. If our journey is to bear rich fruit, we must recognize our parched paralysis, and in an act of trust, surrender to God.

When Christ, the fulfillment of the promises, looks upon the paralytic, he confronts the root cause of suffering: "Your sins are forgiven you" (Lk 5:20). His merciful gaze, when it rests upon a repentant heart, brings life to what was dead and healing to what was broken.

REFLECT

Are you dry and parched, crippled by sorrow? Are you trying to power through every challenge by your own strength? There's great freedom in simply admitting the reality of your spiritual poverty. Write about that here, and open your heart to God's power to strengthen and heal you.

PRAY

*ALMIGHTY GOD, I AM POOR IN
SPIRIT. THANK YOU FOR NOT
EXPECTING ME TO REPAIR MY OWN
BROKENNESS. I COME TO YOU AS A
BEGGAR TODAY, READY FOR YOUR
HEALING, LIFE-GIVING PRESENCE.*

SECOND WEEK OF ADVENT

TUESDAY

EVERYTHING COMES FROM
LOVE, ALL IS ORDAINED FOR THE
SALVATION OF HUMANITY. GOD
DOES NOTHING WITHOUT THIS
GOAL IN MIND.

ST. CATHERINE OF SIENA

GOD'S RELENTLESS LOVE

On our journey through the wilderness of this world, we are prone to wandering astray, much like Israel in the Old Testament. We forget God and chase after idols—and end up feeling lost and alone. But a profound hope penetrates the darkness of isolation and inner sense of hopelessness: while we search for God in fits and starts, God searches for us in relentless love.

Advent is like the final hour before the breaking of the dawn. Our prayer from today's Mass is simple: "Grant, we pray, that we may look forward in joy to the glorious Nativity of Christ." Constantly, the season reminds us to think about where we are directing our attention and invites us to lift our gaze toward those first streaks of light on the horizon.

The coming birth of Christ is both the answer to our longing and the fulfillment of the promises of God woven throughout scripture. Thus, alongside the labor of repentance, we must also study God's Word. Throughout the Old Testament, we find over and over the promises God made to his people in love—promises to come to them, to find them in their misery, and to raise them up.

In our own experience of poverty, we should learn to identify with the sufferings of Israel and with their hope in God's promises. In doing so, we come to understand in a new way the magnitude of Christ's coming. He comes to rescue us, to find us as we have wandered astray, bent beneath the weight of our suffering.

Jesus' parable of the lost sheep beautifully illustrates the astonishing reality of God's unrelenting will to seek and save those who have run away from his love. He leaves the ninety-nine to find the one; none of us is too small to catch his attention. This is the joyful hope we discover when we look to the Nativity. He was born for us, a fact at which we must marvel.

Yet perhaps even more marvelous is this: he was born for *you*.

REFLECT

How do you see yourself as the one lost sheep that the Good Shepherd is willing to pursue? Are you able to recognize yourself as the object of God's relentless love? What would it look like if you took these truths to heart today?

_____

_____

_____

_____

_____

_____

_____

_____

_____

_____

_____

_____

_____

_____

_____

_____

_____

_____

_____

_____

_____

_____

PRAY

JESUS, YOU ARE MY GOOD SHEPHERD.
YOU TRAVELED FAR TO FIND ME WHEN
I WAS LOST. PREPARE MY HEART THIS
ADVENT TO SEE IN YOUR JOURNEY TO
THE MANGER YOUR RELENTLESS LOVE
FOR HUMANITY—AND FOR ME.

DO NOT LOSE HEART, EVEN IF
YOU SHOULD DISCOVER THAT
YOU LACK QUALITIES NECESSARY
FOR THE WORK TO WHICH YOU
ARE CALLED. HE WHO CALLED
YOU WILL NOT DESERT YOU,
BUT THE MOMENT YOU ARE IN
NEED HE WILL STRETCH OUT HIS
SAVING HAND.

ST. ANGELA MERICI

HE GIVES US STRENGTH

Today, with St. Joseph, we confront our inabilities and surrender ourselves to the Lord. God speaks into our weariness with the promises of rest and restoration. In the liturgy for the day, we hear, "He gives power to the faint, and to him who has no might he increases strength. . . . They who wait for the LORD shall renew their strength, they shall mount up with wings like eagles, they shall run and not be weary, they shall walk and not faint" (Is 40:29, 31).

What worries and weariness must have filled Joseph's heart in these days before Mary gave birth! The surprise and confusion her pregnancy must have caused him, his experience of letting go of his own plans for what their life together would look like, and his ongoing discovery of her excellence may very well have caused him to struggle at some level with feelings of unworthiness.

Imagine the obstacles he encountered in his attempts to provide for Mary and her child in the final days before birth. Caesar's call for a census meant Joseph could not offer to Mary the comfort of their own home for childbirth. The long journey likely wore on Joseph as he further encountered his own inability to understand fully Mary's mysterious journey to motherhood. Then, already far from home, Joseph's inability to secure a room at an inn must have been yet another wound to Joseph's spousal and paternal heart.

As Mary tenderly observed the foiled attempts of this righteous man, perhaps she spoke those same words of Isaiah to her husband in his weariness. Perhaps she reminded him of the promises of God, as she reverently received his efforts, even as he felt inadequate and incapable.

Joseph's goodness led him to lay down his life for Mary and her child. We do not know much about the life of Joseph. But we do know that despite his encounters with his own limitations, he persevered and prepared a home in which the life of God could unfold. We hope to do the same in this rich season of preparation. In this, he is a friend and father to us, and so today we "go to Joseph," as the traditional prayer instructs.

REFLECT

It's so tempting to shrink away from an opportunity or a task when we bump up against our own inadequacy. St. Joseph's example reveals a better way: the way of faithful perseverance and reliance on God. How have you seen God's strength revealed in your weakness? What are you facing today or this week that you know you will require a gift of strength from God?

PRAY

ST. JOSEPH, HELP ME IMITATE YOUR PATIENCE WHEN GOD'S PLAN FOR MY LIFE DIVERGES FROM MY DESIRES. INTERCEDE FOR ME AND ASK THAT GOD WOULD STRENGTHEN ME TODAY IN VIRTUE, IN PREPARATION TO RECEIVE JESUS, AND IN THE RESILIENCE TO PERSEVERE IN WHATEVER TASK LIES BEFORE ME.

SECOND WEEK OF ADVENT

THURSDAY

OUR WHOLE BUSINESS IN THIS
LIFE IS TO RESTORE TO HEALTH
THE EYE OF THE HEART WHEREBY
GOD MAY BE SEEN.

ST. AUGUSTINE OF HIPPO

DO YOU SEE HIM?

In the Collect from today's Mass, we beg the Lord to "stir up our hearts" that we would arrive at the Lord's coming "with minds made pure." Advent is a drawing near to God, a journey from far off lands toward the quiet of Bethlehem to look upon the new-born King hidden in a manger.

Unlike the shepherds and Magi or the villagers and towns-people, we already have some sense of what we are approaching as the Nativity nears. Yet Advent invites us always to prepare anew and ever more deeply, so that when we arrive at that cele-bration we would truly *see* him.

In Hebrew, *Bethlehem* means "house of bread." That phrase alone stirs up eucharistic considerations, but we must also note that the English word *manger* is derived from the Latin verb meaning "to eat." The newborn King's cradle was a simple feed-ing trough for the animals in the stable.

There's a vital twofold implication here. First, the eucharis-tic meaning of Christ's coming in the flesh profoundly anchors his later words about the Bread of Life and his work of feeding the multitudes. Second, the Nativity's circumstances indicate a divine preference for hiddenness—under cover of night, in an insignificant town, into profoundly poor surroundings, the King of all creation is born.

Here, we must beg for faith. We recall Christ's words in the Sermon on the Mount: "Blessed are the pure in heart, for they shall see God" (Mt 5:8). By extension, the impure of heart cannot see God, and therefore they are not blessed—yet another reason for our repentance and detachment from worldly goods and goals.

Through the purification of our hearts, our gaze becomes clear, and we begin to recognize God himself, hidden quietly where we would have least expected to find him: in the manger, in the poorest of the poor, and in the Eucharist. Indeed, Advent is truly about sight, vision, and adoration; faith allows us to see that which lies beneath the surface, shimmering in glory right before our eyes.

REFLECT

We long to gaze in awe-filled adoration upon God himself, both hidden *and* revealed to us in seemingly ordinary things. While the Incarnation and the Eucharist are unique types of divine presence, do you think there are other ordinary things in which you can encounter God, hidden yet revealed to eyes of faith? What opportunities do you have to adore him in your everyday life?

_____

_____

_____

_____

_____

_____

_____

_____

_____

_____

_____

_____

PRAY

_ALMIGHTY GOD, I BEG TODAY THAT
YOU WOULD OPEN THE EYES OF MY
HEART. GRANT ME FAITH TO SEE
WHAT LIES BEYOND THE SURFACE:
THE GLORY OF YOUR PRESENCE ALL
AROUND ME._

SECOND WEEK OF ADVENT

FRIDAY

WATCH THEREFORE, FOR YOU
KNOW NEITHER THE DAY NOR
THE HOUR.

MATTHEW 25:13

WAITING FOR
THE BRIDEGROOM

The liturgical rhythm of the season, so very instructive of the great mysteries of our faith, continues to draw us back to the steady theme: "Grant that your people, we pray, almighty God, may be ever watchful for the coming of your Only Begotten Son," that "we may hasten, alert and with lighted lamps, to meet him when he comes."

This prayer from today's Mass calls to mind that rich image from Matthew 25. There, Jesus tells the parable of the ten virgins who keep vigil in anticipation of the bridegroom's approach. The parable, framed around a wedding, reminds us that God comes to espouse his people to himself in a new and everlasting covenant.

Nuptial language pervades the entirety of sacred scripture, and Christ's identification as the divine Bridegroom is a tremendously beautiful and significant aspect of the gospels. While a wedding between a man and a woman brings great joy, every marriage actually points to the deeper mystery of the wedding between Christ and his people. The union of the Bride-Church and the Lamb, creature and Creator, is the form and finality of every other marriage.

Yet our celebration of this divine marriage, tasted here on earth and fulfilled completely in heaven, doesn't always stir our hearts or invigorate the Church the way it should. Perhaps the parable offers some explanation of why this is the case in a detail that often eludes commentary: *all* of the virgins become drowsy and fall asleep.

This is somewhat consoling. It indicates that there is a sort of inevitability about the flesh's imperfection and our tendency to become distracted by the world around us, even to the point of lethargy. Like it or not, the concept of the wedding feast of the Lamb sometimes does not move us deeply. It shouldn't surprise us when we are also somewhat unmoved by the advent of the Lamb in his first visible and gentlest form—as a baby in the manger.

Even so, five of the virgins in the parable, despite growing drowsy in the waiting, remained well prepared. They brought extra oil for their lamps, aware that the vigil might be long and demanding. Traditionally, the oil is seen to represent the works of charity accompanied by the type of fasting that hones our longing for the things of heaven. How very sensible is the practice of charity and penance as a remedy for lukewarm and tepid hearts!

REFLECT

Do you feel yourself growing drowsy or distracted as you wait on the Lord? Reflect on some intentional acts of charity and fasting you can do to help you remain vigilant.

_____

_____

_____

_____

_____

_____

_____

PRAY

*LORD, MY FLESH IS WEAK. I GROW
SLEEPY AND INATTENTIVE AS I WAIT
FOR YOUR PRESENCE. BLESS ME WITH
THE GRACE TO REMAIN SPIRITUALLY
ALERT, EVEN WHEN MY BODY GROWS
WEARY.*

SECOND WEEK OF ADVENT

SATURDAY

WHAT A JOYOUS MYSTERY IS
YOUR PRESENCE WITHIN ME, IN
THAT INTIMATE SANCTUARY OF
MY SOUL WHERE I CAN ALWAYS
FIND YOU.

ST. ELIZABETH OF THE TRINITY

PREPARED FOR GOD'S INDWELLING PRESENCE

A twofold theme emerges at this point in our journey. On one side, our focus is on the inner room of our hearts; we are called to prepare a place for the Lord within as the works of charity and penance enkindle the interior flame of love. On the other side, our watchfulness attends to the horizon, from which we await the approach of the One who later proclaims, "I am the light of the world" (Jn 8:12).

Advent is thus the encounter of two lights: that fire of love that burns within us and the same fire of love that comes to us from without. Our Advent each year is something like an annual pilgrimage as Spirit-inflamed hearts from across the earth converge on that piercing scene in Bethlehem.

Mary is the first to intimately know a beautiful truth about how God comes to us. She enjoys a special season in which the Light that approaches all of creation is first hidden within her womb.

The indwelling presence of God may very well be the least understood and most exciting fact of our Christian existence. Our minds simply cannot grasp the fullness of the mystery that God chooses to hide himself within creation, that he chooses the humble and broken heart of the believer as his home.

To live in a full awareness of this breathtaking fact would utterly reshape our lives down to the tiniest circumstances of every moment. Our frenetic pace renders us forgetful of this fact, and we resign ourselves to living "up at the surface" and outside the deep gift of interior communion with God. Each year we return to Advent with the desire to live more deeply. No greater figure comes to our aid in this area than Mary.

However mundane or fantastic, simple or mystical were her days of expectation, they were woven with the real and felt presence of the Word Incarnate growing within her. In some ways, our days are not so different, for God dwells in the center of the baptized soul. Today, we beg Mary's assistance to become more aware of this stunning fact that God comes to us and makes a home with us (see John 14:23).

REFLECT

It is not easy to comprehend that God makes his home in our souls. How might it change the way you think, interact, and spend your time if you could hold the truth of God's indwelling presence in your mind throughout the day?

_____

_____

_____

_____

_____

_____

_____

_____

_____

PRAY

*MOST GRACIOUS VIRGIN MARY, YOU
EXPERIENCED GOD'S INDWELLING
PRESENCE IN A SPECIAL WAY. HELP
ME EXPERIENCE GOD'S INDWELLING
PRESENCE IN MY OWN SOUL, FOR
THE TRANSFORMATION OF MY HEART,
MIND, AND ACTIONS.*

THIRD WEEK
OF ADVENT

NEARNESS

THIRD WEEK OF ADVENT

SUNDAY

DRAW NEAR TO GOD AND HE
WILL DRAW NEAR TO YOU.

JAMES 4:8

HE IS NEAR

When a family prepares to host a beloved friend, the home bustles with energy and anticipation. Smiles rise over quickened steps and hearts. The announcement that their guest is near stirs cries of hopeful joy, especially among the children. Such is meant to be today's mood, on a Sunday rightly called *Gaudete Sunday,* so named for the invitation to rejoice issued in the entrance antiphon for Mass: "Rejoice in the Lord always; again I say, rejoice. Indeed, the Lord is near."

Today the Church celebrates the nearness of her Savior. As the invitation to spiritual preparation crescendos in the liturgy, so too does the urgency of preparation for the concrete and material celebrations that approach. Christmas is near, which means the last-minute shopping, baking, wrapping, and cleaning all start to weigh down upon us.

At this point in the season, we always stand teetering between a fuller engagement of the real point and purpose of Advent or getting swept away in the often overwhelming material preparations.

Gaudete Sunday invites us to pause in the midst of the activity and breathe deeply. The material celebrations of Christmas come and go each year. But if we let the rich invitation of Advent seep to the core of our hearts, we actually find ourselves freed to prepare more intentionally and celebrate more fully with family and friends.

When the birth of Christ is the actual impetus for our celebrations, and thus our preparation, then the pressure to get our celebrations "just right" this year eases. Whether we host or are hosted, a deepened heart for Christ means that we bring to the celebrations a greater capacity to welcome the birth of faith in our homes and gatherings.

The shopping, baking, wrapping, and cleaning can actually all be undertaken with a wish to not only honor those with whom we celebrate but also to honor the One who causes our very celebration.

He is near. As we prepare, we rejoice, and with faith we orient every detail of the days to come toward him.

REFLECT

Today, think carefully about the traditions and activities that you have planned for this Christmas season. How do they amplify Jesus' nearness? How do they feed your anticipation of his arrival? If they are a burden and a distraction, how can you reorient them and your own heart toward Christ?

_____

_____

_____

_____

_____

_____

_____

_____

_____

_____

_____

PRAY

DEAR JESUS, FILL ME WITH A SENSE
OF YOUR NEARNESS DURING THIS
ADVENT SEASON. MAY THE JOY OF
YOUR IMMINENT ARRIVAL INFUSE
EVERY EVENT AND CELEBRATION.

THIRD WEEK OF ADVENT

MONDAY

THE WHOLE EARTH IS A LIVING
ICON OF THE FACE OF GOD.

ST. JOHN DAMASCENE

SEEK HIS FACE

Flowing from yesterday's call to regain perspective in light of the nearness of Christ, the liturgy today invites us to recognize the relationship between our lives on earth and our heavenly destiny. Indeed, the Prayer after Communion implores the Lord that the Sacrifice of the Mass would bless us in a crowning fashion: "May these mysteries, O Lord, in which we have participated, profit us, we pray, for even now, as we walk amid passing things, you teach us by them to love the things of heaven and hold fast to what endures."

While our faith calls us to put to death in ourselves the pattern of fallen ways and to abolish disordered attachments to created goods, it does not call us to hate creation or despise the order of nature. Rather, by faith we recognize the innate goodness of creation as authored by the One who is truly good.

Creation has an inherently pedagogical structure—it was designed to teach us about the Creator. So our engagement with created goods, when purified by faith and sanctified by grace, perfects our ability to understand the pilgrim journey homeward *and* to enjoy it. What a word of hope in the midst of the year's most materialistic stretch!

Every year there's a risk that the meaning of Christmas will be drowned out by stress, greed, and conflict. It shouldn't surprise us that the annual celebration of God's gift of salvation born into our lives would so easily be eclipsed by our tendency to focus our eyes and hearts on lesser gifts.

The logic of gift-giving, hospitality, and celebratory gatherings can and must be integrated into the framework of grace and true faith. This is the framework that upholds the entire created order, revealing humanity's destiny of everlasting happiness. Yes, we walk amid passing things, but we do so with hearts set on the everlasting gift. We most fully celebrate within creation and using created elements when we welcome faith's purifying and ordering influence over our seasonal activities.

Today, we beg for faith's increase. In our moments of reflection, we beg the Holy Spirit to anoint our day not only with the ability to get our many tasks accomplished but also with a greater docility to the promptings of God, so that in the noise and busyness of the day we will seek and find his face.

REFLECT

What are some ways you can "welcome faith's purifying and ordering influence" into your Christmas planning and celebration this year?

PRAY

*FATHER IN HEAVEN, HELP ME SEE
HOW ETERNITY PERMEATES MY
EVERYDAY ACTIVITIES. MAY I AND
ALL THOSE WITH WHOM I SPEND
CHRISTMAS THIS YEAR SEEK YOUR
FACE IN ALL OF OUR ACTIVITIES.
MAY WE DEVELOP EYES TO SEE THE
GIFT-GIVING AND THE CELEBRATIONS
WITHIN THE FRAMEWORK OF TRUE
FAITH.*

THIRD WEEK OF ADVENT

TUESDAY

IN ADORING OUR SAVIOR'S
BIRTH, IT IS OUR ORIGIN THAT WE
CELEBRATE. CHRIST'S TEMPORAL
GENERATION IS THE SOURCE
OF THE CHRISTIAN PEOPLE,
THE BIRTH OF HIS MYSTICAL
BODY. ALL OF US ENCOUNTER
IN THIS MYSTERY A NEW BIRTH
IN CHRIST.

ST. LEO THE GREAT

SOMETHING NEW

The coming of Christ was an utterly new event in the history of salvation. Nothing like it had ever happened before, and nothing has been the same since. The coming of Christ is marked radically by the character of *newness*—even re-creation.

The Collect at today's Mass articulates this reality as the Church prays for deeper conversion, and we cannot help but recall our earlier engagement of repentance: "O God, who through your Only Begotten Son have made us a new creation, look kindly, we pray, on the handiwork of your mercy, and at your Son's coming, cleanse us from every stain of the old way of life."

The coming of the Son of God is more than a singular historical event. Ever since the Incarnation, Christ continues to come to us over and over again. He comes to us in prayer, in sacrament, and in the poor. Christ will also come in a final, culminating fashion at the end of time. The character of newness marks each and all of these comings of Christ; as he proclaims in the vision from Revelation, "Behold, I make all things new" (Rv 21:5). Where Christ comes, there is always something new.

We do well to recall this fact as Christmas nears. Yes, we will engage in familiar patterns at Christmas. We will (hopefully) finish our preparations, gather with friends and family, worship the Lord, open gifts, feast, and celebrate. Sometimes, unfortunately, these celebrations can feel stale or perfunctory. Other times, they can be agonizing and painful, especially when we have lost loved ones or when brokenness and division riddle our families.

It is always right there—wherever we feel the tug and pull of the fallen, old way of life—that Christ comes. He comes into our darkness, into our frailty, into our sorrow, into our isolation. However we find ourselves feeling about the celebrations to come, today we recognize the newness of Christ's coming. We ask for the grace to welcome it, especially into the places that have grown cold, hidden, and dark. He comes to us there to cleanse us and, over and over again, to make us new.

REFLECT

The newness that Jesus brought (and still brings today) is a source of perpetual hope. What in your life needs to be made new?

_____

_____

_____

_____

_____

_____

_____

_____

_____

_____

_____

_____

_____

_____

_____

_____

_____

_____

_____

_____

_____

PRAY

*ALMIGHTY GOD, THANK YOU
FOR THE NEW WORK YOU DID IN
SENDING YOUR BELOVED SON TO
OUR SUFFERING WORLD. MAY THIS
ADVENT BE A SEASON OF NEWNESS IN
MY OWN LIFE AS I LOOK TO YOU TO
BRING HOPE, HEALING, AND PEACE.*

THIRD WEEK OF ADVENT

WEDNESDAY

HE HEALS THE BROKENHEARTED,

AND BINDS UP THEIR WOUNDS.

PSALM 147:3

AT HOME WITH CHRIST

As a consequence of the Fall, human nature is wounded by sin. Trapped beneath the weight of our own fallenness, we tend to perpetuate our woundedness by layering sin upon hidden sin. Our culture suggests that to ask for help is to show weakness and to be weak is to fail. So we force ourselves to live like soldiers broken on the battlefield; we hurriedly stitch ourselves up, cover the wounds, and get back to work.

But this is no way to live, grievously wounded, limping through life, concealing our pain from the world and each other. We survive like this until one day someone accidentally touches a hidden wound. All at once, the searing pain bursts forth, and we display the truth for all to see: we are not well.

This is our shared human condition, and it is precisely into this broken world that Christ comes. In the words of today's Collect: "Grant, we pray, almighty God, that the coming solemnity of your Son may bestow healing upon us in this present life." In God's kindness, this healing gift is offered freely, not imposed upon us.

St. Joseph, we might speculate, learned how to welcome this gift. We can only imagine the ways in which Christ might have ministered to Joseph in those hidden years at Nazareth. Joseph himself, subject to sin and sharing with us a wounded human nature, must have experienced the very presence of Christ drawing his weaknesses and wounds from darkness to light. What was it like, year after year, for Joseph to receive—in his own poverty—the loving gaze of Jesus Christ? Joseph may well have been the first to welcome the healing power of God into a wounded human heart.

Christ's ministry is for healing, as he himself proclaims in the gospel: "Go and tell John what you have seen and heard: the blind receive their sight, the lame walk, lepers are cleansed, and the deaf hear, the dead are raised up, the poor have good news preached to them" (Lk 7:22). With St. Joseph, let us welcome this powerful gift today.

REFLECT

In our most honest moments, we see that we desperately need healing, but we often don't know where to start. Reflect on what it might look like in your own life to be, like St. Joseph, "at home" with Christ—comfortable in his presence and honest about your need for the healing only he can bring to your wounded heart.

_____

_____

_____

_____

_____

_____

_____

_____

_____

PRAY

*BLESSED ST. JOSEPH, YOU KNOW
WHAT IT MEANS TO BE AT HOME
WITH CHRIST, WHOSE VERY PRESENCE
REVEALS OUR WOUNDS AND BRINGS
HEALING. AS I MEDITATE ON THE
NEARNESS OF CHRIST THIS ADVENT,
HELP ME HAVE THE COURAGE TODAY
TO OPEN MY HEART TO HIS HEALING
PRESENCE.*

THIRD WEEK OF ADVENT

THURSDAY

I DEVOUTLY ADORE YOU, O
HIDDEN DEITY, TRULY HIDDEN
BENEATH THESE APPEARANCES.

ST. THOMAS AQUINAS

HIDDEN, YET REVEALED

As the Church's anticipation of Christ's Nativity grows and our journey rises toward Bethlehem, we recognize an innate tension within our pilgrim state. Christ's coming, which we celebrate annually, has already happened historically; yet, it is prolonged and encountered anew through the Holy Sacrifice of the Mass, and we also wait in joyful hope for Christ's Second Coming. At Christmas, we thus celebrate something that has passed, is repeated again and again, and is still to come.

Our annual reentry into these mysteries always increases our awareness of that which is already accomplished as well as our awareness of how we share in it at present. The gift of Christ's abiding presence turns us toward the horizon of heaven. Therein lies the thrill of faithful living; we are never quite there, but as we move and live more deeply, our hearts expand and our joy increases along with our longing for the "ever after" of Paradise.

If Christmas Eve contains the first glance, as it were, of the newborn King who is Lord and Savior, Advent stirs a readiness for that moment's approach. In a sense, Christmas must always be about adoration. That moment of coming face-to-face with God in the flesh must result in an outpouring of praise, thanksgiving, wonder, awe, and ultimately, worship.

As we ponder adoration, we recall the eucharistic details of Jesus' birth in Bethlehem, a little child laid in a manger. Christmas and the Eucharist are woven closely together, for Christ repeats the pattern of his quiet and hidden entrance into creation at every Mass. Throughout our churches across the globe, Christ hides himself under small and simple created elements. God's preference for hiddenness provokes our search for him.

We worship what appears to us as a baby, or a wafer of bread—but what faith tells us is so much more. St. Francis of Assisi saw this, marveled at it, and was so pierced by it that he wrote a letter to his entire order imploring them to worship the Lord in the Eucharist.

In lieu of our usual "Reflect" prompt and short prayer, spend time with this prayer from St. Francis. Make his prayer your own as you ponder and write about the God who, in hiding himself in ordinary created things, reveals and gives himself to us.

Let the whole of mankind tremble,
the whole world shake, and the heavens exult
when Christ, the Son of the living God,
is [present] on the altar in the hands of a priest.
O admirable heights and sublime lowliness!
O sublime humility! O humble sublimity!
That the Lord of the universe,
God and the Son of God,
so humbles himself that for our salvation
he hides himself under the little form of bread!
Look, brothers, at the humility of God
and pour out your hearts before him!
Humble yourselves, as well,
that you may be exalted by him.
Therefore,
hold back nothing of yourselves for yourselves
so that he who gives himself totally to you
may receive you totally.

THIRD WEEK OF ADVENT

FRIDAY

FASTING IS THE SUPPORT OF
OUR SOUL: IT GIVES US WINGS
TO ASCEND ON HIGH.

ST. JOHN CHRYSOSTOM

MAKE SPACE FOR YOUR SOUL'S DEEPEST LONGING

How difficult must have been those final days before the Nativity as Mary and Joseph made the arduous journey to Bethlehem. Along with the anxiety and uncertainty, the journey was likely marked by hunger, thirst, and exhaustion. Yet, when Christ was finally born and they adored him in awe, we can imagine that they looked tenderly at one another with a single sentiment: "It was all worth it." The sufferings of Mary and Joseph and the eventual sufferings of Christ—all borne for the sake of God's great work of redemption—frame our own consideration of penance as we enter this Friday of Advent.

When we fast, we curb the appetites of the flesh and create space for the deeper longings of the soul to expand. Bodily hunger and thirst, when united to the sacrificial offering of Christ on the Cross, bring about manifold fruits.

Fasting brings us into solidarity with those who live in want, a matter which spurs gratitude for our blessedness and fraternal concern for the poor. Penance lifts our attention from the pursuit of comfort among creatures to adoration of the Creator who also comforts (see Zechariah 1:17; Acts 9:31). It clarifies our vision and prepares us to meet God. Our bodily hunger and thirst have analogical counterparts on the spiritual plane: in a penitential spirit, these surges of yearning increase our desire for the Bread of Life and Living Water promised by Christ.

In each of these ways, bodily penance reminds us that we are "seeking a homeland" (Heb 11:14) and that this life is not the whole story. Throughout the year, Friday turns our attention to the Passion and teaches us to see, to want, and to partake in a way that is ordered not toward our own natural gratification but toward the kingdom.

The Prayer after Communion at today's Mass reminds us of the special help that the Eucharist brings us. In the same moment, it pinpoints the source of our hope as we approach the Nativity, especially as we grapple with our own hunger and thirst: "Replenished by the food of spiritual nourishment, we humbly beseech you, O Lord, that, through our partaking in this mystery, you may teach us to judge wisely the things of earth and hold firm to the things of heaven."

REFLECT

Humans have a complicated (and sometimes competing) collection of desires. Fasting is one tool available to us for our task of ordering our desires toward God. Today, reflect on your experiences of trying to bring order to your desires. Which desires typically distract you from God? Which desires seem to form in your heart a natural path toward him?

PRAY

*HEAVENLY FATHER, AS I TRAVEL
THIS PILGRIM PATH TO MY TRUE
HOME, HELP ME MAKE ALLIES OF
MY DESIRES. MAY MY APPETITES,
RIGHTLY ORDERED, SERVE TO
HEIGHTEN MY LONGING FOR YOU.*

THIRD WEEK OF ADVENT

SATURDAY

THE HOLY SPIRIT COMES WHERE
HE IS LOVED, WHERE HE IS
INVITED, WHERE HE IS EXPECTED.

ST. BONAVENTURE

ANTICIPATION

In the time leading up to the birth of Christ, Mary and Joseph must have spent time wondering what this child would be like. They probably shared ideas and hopes, wondered how his personality would develop, and imagined what it would be like for their home to be filled with new sounds and life. Their home at Nazareth must have been filled with the music of their shared delight in anticipation of Jesus' birth.

What was it like for Mary to feel the child move in her womb? To let the Holy Spirit stir her anticipation of meeting this little one? How often during those months did she return to the words of the angel? "He will be great, and will be called the Son of the Most High . . . and of his kingdom there will be no end" (Lk 1:32–33). How she must have wondered at the meaning of such lofty words, and how she must have longed to see the face of the One so mighty.

Regardless of how much she knew of what was to come, how humbled and honored she must have felt to recognize that this divine King's first months in our midst were spent within her own womb, that she would hold him lovingly to her breast before his might would be known to the world.

What must have gone through Joseph's mind as he watched Mary quietly ponder these matters, as he saw the delicate smile crease her face as her mind's eye glimpsed the joy that was to come? Did she notice his attentive observation and lift her eyes to his? Imagine those moments, mostly wordless, as smiles passed from one to the other and the warmth of expectation joined their hearts.

Wonderfully, we realize, none of their expectations could ever measure up to the sheer grace that awaited them in the years to come. In quite a real way, this is also where we find ourselves. We ponder scripture, we remember the mighty works of God, and we look forward in great hope to that which is to come. With Mary and Joseph at this moment in Advent, we look forward with hope, and we recognize with delight that we still have only the slightest glimmer of all the good that God has prepared for us.

REFLECT

Write about your experience over the past week of focusing your attention on the nearness of Christ.

_____

_____

_____

_____

_____

_____

_____

_____

_____

PRAY

LORD JESUS CHRIST, I AM FILLED WITH ANTICIPATION OF YOUR ARRIVAL. EVEN AS I CELEBRATE YOUR NATIVITY, I LOOK AHEAD TO THE COMPLETE FULFILLMENT OF YOUR BEAUTIFUL PLAN TO REDEEM AND RESTORE YOUR PEOPLE.

FOURTH WEEK
OF ADVENT

EMMANUEL

FOURTH WEEK OF ADVENT

O COME, LET US ADORE HIM,
CHRIST THE LORD.

"O COME, ALL YE FAITHFUL"

SILENCE AND ADORATION

In this final week of Advent, two themes intersect to bring us to Christmas: silence and adoration.

First, we marvel at the Lord's use of, and even preference for, silence. The book of Wisdom foreshadowed the surprising silence that accompanied the Incarnation: "For while gentle silence enveloped all things, and night in its swift course was now half gone, your all-powerful word leaped from heaven, from the royal throne, into the midst of the land that was doomed" (Ws 18:14–15). Indeed, under both the cover of night and the cloak of poverty the Word takes his first breath and quietly breaks the night's silence with a human cry.

O come, let us adore him! We come with the eyes of our hearts focused and free, yearning and searching for the "something more" that stirs our deepest ache. We find it neither in triumphant displays of power nor in the stars above nor the sea below. Rather, we find the answer to our questions and the satisfaction of our longing hearts quietly resting in a manger, out in back behind a crowded inn. What a lesson about the search for God!

Visitors to Bethlehem who were overly occupied with themselves or their own affairs may have walked right through the town with nothing but disdain for its simplicity, for their hearts were so hardened by worldly concerns as to find little worth noticing in this small scene on the margins. Only the humble heart, the person with eyes to see and a willingness to believe despite the failing of the senses, could come to the manger and truly *see*.

We beg the Lord for this posture of heart as we conclude our journey. At the manger, we will find each year a baby with the noblest destiny, God himself enfleshed and resting in our very midst. In the silent beholding, we are invited to be more than mere spectators. In beholding, we recognize what is here hidden, and we worship.

As we worship and we adore him, something happens within us. When we give God what is his due, we are drawn out of ourselves and beyond our own limits into communion, into relationship, into Love. Worship has no further end than offering back to God our whole lives, a rendering of praise and thanksgiving in grateful and humble recognition of his Lordship and our dependence upon him. Only in this activity that produces nothing (in the world's assessment) do we actually find what we have sought down empty paths, guided by partial desires and left only partially satisfied.

As he has from the beginning, God comes to us in silence, under the quiet cover of a dark night, to draw us out of our own futility and into himself. As that beautiful and heartrending process begins each Christmas, we bow our hearts and, wide-eyed and smiling, we adore him.

Isaiah prophesied this great day, and Matthew's gospel points to its fulfillment in Jesus Christ: "The people who sat in darkness have seen a great light, and for those who sat in the region and shadow of death light has dawned" (Mt 4:16). Indeed, the weight of sin crushed the people of Israel for generations until it seemed that the cycle could never be broken. Whether we like it or not, our lives too tend to drift into this darkness over and over again. As life and our daily concerns weigh upon us, despite our best efforts, we too can become crushed and fall into despair. But once again, this is precisely why Jesus came.

The first passages of John's gospel may very well be the most powerful in all of scripture. For centuries, these words were proclaimed at the end of every single Mass as a reminder to all who came to enter into the silence, to adore God, and to worship. They were proclaimed as a reminder that though God has entered into our world and redeemed it, the battle is not finished until the final day. These words concluded the act of worship to fortify the hearts of believers as they returned to everyday life, and they are well worth our prayerful consideration:

> In the beginning was the Word, and the Word was with God, and the Word was God. He was in the beginning with God; all things were made through him, and without him was not anything made that was made. In him was life, and the life was the light of men. The light shines in the darkness, and the darkness has not overcome it. . . .
>
> The true light that enlightens every man was coming into the world. . . .
>
> And the Word became flesh and dwelt among us, full of grace and truth; we have beheld his glory, glory as of the only-begotten Son from the Father. . . . And from his fulness have we all received, grace upon grace. (Jn 1:1–5, 9, 14, 16)

In this final week of Advent, as loud as our lives may become, rests the invitation of God to draw near. The silence we seek is not so much a departure from the world but a living more deeply within it. A pause here, a prayerful few minutes there, a turn of our thoughts toward the center of the soul where God dwells, a visit to the Blessed Sacrament, a glance at the manger, a few moments with scripture, a whisper of prayer—and we are brought back to what is most deeply beautiful and true. Jesus' very title, Emmanuel, is our consolation, for it literally means "God with us."

Recognition of his coming to be with us is the culmination of this Advent journey, which now comes to a close. As we allow silence and adoration to converge, we stand in awe of God as that dark night is pierced by an endless light. As we let that awe fully saturate our souls, out of silent worship our praise expands. Under the sway of grace, we slip into the type of song that makes all people wonder at our joy, peace, and love. As we sing, drawn ever closer to God, our longing is to bring all the nations to see and adore with us. We cannot help but proclaim, with the words of that treasured hymn, "O come, let us adore him!"

As we do so, converging at the manger with stranger and friend alike, we also discover that this journey is really not over at all. The light dawns again—and now we celebrate, please God, with hearts more fully his than ever before.

REFLECT AND PRAY

St. John Paul II tells us that "our whole life should be an 'advent,' in vigilant expectation of Christ's final coming. . . . Advent is then a period of intense training that directs us decisively to the One who has already come, who will come, and who continuously comes" (General Audience, December 18, 2002).

As you embark on these final days of Advent, take some time to gather the graces of the previous weeks. Where is your heart now? What has changed from where you began? What can you do to take this season of "intense training" beyond Advent and Christmas, into the rest of your life?

The final week of Advent is not always a full week. In fact, though there are always four Sundays in Advent, the number of days between the last Sunday of Advent and Christmas day varies from zero to six.

Because of that, we have provided a unified "Reflect and Pray" section that you can work through at your own pace, regardless of how many days of the Advent season remain.

We suggest reading the prayer provided here each day between now and Christmas (whether that's just a single day or an entire week). On the pages following the prayer you'll find four reflection questions and plenty of journaling space so that you may reflect more deeply on all that you've learned and experienced this Advent season.

JESUS,
I LONG FOR YOUR LOVE IN MY LIFE;
HELP ME HEAR, SEE, AND KNOW YOU.
SET MY HEART ABLAZE WITH JOY
WHEN I FIND YOU, SO THAT I MAY
GLORIFY YOU WITH MY LIFE.

How will you foster vigilant *watchfulness*, always ready to run to Christ wherever he presents himself?

_____

_____

_____

_____

_____

_____

_____

_____

_____

_____

_____

_____

_____

What habits of *preparation* will you take up to keep your heart attuned to eternity, even as you live in this between time, surrounded by everyday cares and tasks?

How will you celebrate the *nearness* of Jesus and the indwelling presence of his Spirit?

_____

_____

_____

_____

_____

_____

_____

_____

_____

_____

_____

_____

How will you worship and adore *Emmanuel*, this God who wills to be with us, hidden yet revealed in history, manifest in the poor, awaiting us in the Mass and Eucharistic Adoration?

FR. JOHN BURNS is a priest of the Archdiocese of Milwaukee and author of the bestselling book *Lift Up Your Heart: A 10-Day Personal Retreat with St. Francis de Sales*. Ordained in 2010, he has served as an associate pastor and pastor in Milwaukee, Wisconsin, as well as an adjunct professor of moral theology at the Sacred Heart Seminary and School of Theology. He completed a doctorate in moral theology at the Pontifical University of the Holy Cross in Rome in 2019. His doctoral research focused on the theology of healing through forgiveness.

Burns speaks at conferences, preaches missions, and directs retreats throughout the country. He works extensively with the Sisters of Life and St. Mother Teresa's Missionaries of Charity, and he has given retreats, conferences, and spiritual direction for the sisters in Africa, Europe, and the United States.

VALERIE DELGADO is a Catholic painter, a digital artist, and the owner of Pax.Beloved. She illustrated the book *ABC Get to Know the Saints with Me* by Caroline Perkins.

She lives in the Houston, Texas, area.

www.paxbeloved.com
Instagram: @pax.valerie

Celebrate Advent
WITH YOUR ENTIRE PARISH OR GROUP!

FREE *Adore* companion resources and videos are available to enhance your Advent experience and make it simple to customize for use in a parish, small group, or classroom setting.

Visit **www.avemariapress.com/adore** to find:

- *Adore Leader's Guide,*

- weekly reflection videos,

- pulpit and bulletin announcements,

- downloadable flyers, posters, and digital graphics,

- and more!